CITIES OF
TOMORROW AND
THE CITY TO COME

CITIES OF TOMORROW AND THE CITY TO COME

A THEOLOGY OF
URBAN LIFE

NOAH TOLY

GENE L. GREEN, SERIES EDITOR

ZONDERVAN

Cities of Tomorrow and the City to Come

Copyright © 2015 by Noah J. Toly

This title is also available as a Zondervan ebook. Visit www.zondervan.com/ebooks.

Requests for information should be addressed to:

Zondervan, 3900 *Sparks Dr. SE, Grand Rapids, Michigan* 49546

Library of Congress Cataloging-in-Publication Data

Toly, Noah.
    Cities of tomorrow and the city to come : a theology of urban life / Noah Toly.
       pages cm.–(Ordinary theology)
      ISBN 978-0-310-51601-9 (softcover)
      1. Cities and towns–Religious aspects–Christianity. I. Title.
BR115.C45T65 2015
270.8'3091732–dc23
                                          2014042614

Cover design: Mikah Kandros
Interior design: Beth Shagene
Editorial: Madison Trammel, Peter Vogel, Bob Hudson
Printed in the United States of America

15 16 17 18 19 20 21 22 23 24 /DCI/ 20 19 18 17 16 15 14 13 12 11 10 9 8 7 6 5 4 3 2 1

*To my Wheaton in Chicago students
and to all those
who seek the welfare of the city*

CONTENTS

FOREWORD TO THE ORDINARY THEOLOGY SERIES

Gene L. Green

O*rdinary theology*. These two words together sound like an oxy-moron. We're accustomed to thinking about "theology" as the stiff and stifling stuff found in ponderous tomes written by Christian scholars in ivory towers, places far removed from our ordinary lives. We live on the street, in our homes, in places of business, in schools, in gyms, and in churches. What does theology have to do with the ordinary affairs of our daily lives?

We want to bring the Bible into our lives, to be sure, and we attend church to learn about God's Word. We read our favorite passages and wonder how ancient stories about Noah on the water or Jesus on the water relate to the checkout at the grocery store, the hours at work, the novel we read for pleasure, the sicknesses we endure, the votes we cast, or the bed. How do we construct a bridge between the biblical worlds and the twenty-first-century world as we seek to follow Jesus faithfully? The distance between our local shopping center and Paul's forum in Athens (Acts 17) seems like an unbridgeable canyon. What does the Bible have to do with the wonderful or difficult realities we face on the baseball field or in the city? How do we receive God's Word, which is truly for all people, at all times, in all places?

It's an old question, one the church has been asking for centuries. The Bible is a historical document with contemporary relevance. But we're also aware that it doesn't seem to speak directly to many situations we face. There is no obvious biblical view of nuclear war, a kind of destruction unknown in the ancient world. What about epidemics such as AIDS, an unknown disease in the ancient world? The Noah story describes a dramatic climate change, but does that cataclysm have anything to do with global warming today? Through the centuries, Christians have understood that the Bible cannot be simply proof-texted in all life's situations. Yet we still believe that the Bible is God's word for us in our complex world. Enter theology.

The word *theology* comes from a couple of Greek terms: *theos* and *logos*. *Theos* means "God" and *logos* means "word." Simply stated, theology is words that express thoughts about God. We hold beliefs about God such as "God is love" (1 John 4:8). We understand that Jesus died for our sins and that we have a hope that transcends the grave because of the resurrection of Christ. All these are theological statements. We have received Christian theology through our parents, church, and Scripture reading, and we attempt to find how biblically based belief relates to our lives. We do theology as we take Scripture and our inherited theology and seek to work out what God is saying about the issues of today. Every Christian is a theologian.

Ordinary theology is, really, just another way to say *theology*. The expression emphasizes how theology is part of the ordinary stuff of daily life. Food is a theological topic. We can think about buying food, the need for food, those without food, selling food. What does the Bible have to say about food supply, hunger, and generosity? To ask that question is to think theologically about food. What about government welfare or foreign aid? We can think through the whole of Scripture and apply its perspectives and teachings to such issues. This is theology. And it is something every Christian can and must do. We believe that the gospel is relevant not only to our inner life, but to life in the world. The road we travel as ordinary Christians is to do "ordinary theology" as we work God's message into all aspects of daily life.

The Ordinary Theology Series has a few goals. The first is to take up the common issues of daily life and think through them theologically. But another purpose of the series is to invite you to develop your skills as a theologian. These small books are examples of theological method but also a welcome into the necessary, challenging, and joyous task of doing theology. We're all called to follow the example of the first great Christian theologian whose day job was netting fish for a living. Peter did not receive training in the rabbinic schools as had Paul, yet he was the one who first understood and stated that Jesus was the Christ, the Son of the Living God (Matt. 16:16). He also opened the door of faith to the Gentiles as he came to understand that God accepts every person, regardless of ethnicity (Acts 10). Each of us can make a theological contribution to the church, our family, our community, and our own life. For your sake and the sake of others, be a theologian.

One final word about format. Each chapter begins with a story, and theological reflection follows. Theology happens in the place where Scripture meets us on the road where "life is lived tensely, where thought has its birth in conflict and concern, where choices are made and decisions are carried out."[1] We go to Scripture and the deep well of Christian theology as we develop our theology in the place where we find ourselves. God is concerned about people and places and does not ask us to divorce ourselves from them as we follow and serve Christ. And he gives us guidance on how to do that. So, enjoy the read! And again: be the theologian.

WHAT HAS CHICAGO TO DO WITH JERUSALEM?

A Preface on Learning, Faith, and Urban Life

When Gene Green first asked me to contribute to this series, I was astonished by the timing. I had just—I mean *just*—finished telling a friend about a recent lunch with one of the foremost urbanists of our time. This urbanist, one of the world's most influential scholars of cities and urban life, had requested a lunch with me during a conference we were both attending. Her invitation was the kind that you don't turn down. Little did I know when I accepted it, though, that our meeting would focus on a discussion of faith and learning and, more specifically, the relationship between Christian faith and how we come to understand contemporary urban life.

Over lunch we discussed her most recent big project and my latest work, and then she asked this question: "Now, Noah, I recently wrote a letter recommending you for a year-long opportunity to study theology and religious ethics. I'm really glad that worked out. But I have one question, and as someone who recommended you, I think I am entitled to ask it: Why? Why would an urbanist like you want to study theology and ethics? Why would you spend your sabbatical doing *that*? I mean, I understand why clergy would want to study these things, but why would an urbanist want to do that? I understand why Rowan Williams would want to think theologically, but why you?" At the time, Rowan Williams was the Archbishop of Canterbury and head of the Anglican Communion. The scholar I was dining with had apparently met Williams on several occasions and, despite their many differences on religion, very much admired him. She understood why Williams, an eminent theological scholar and professional minister of the gospel, would want to study theology and religious ethics. But why me?

Why me indeed! The answer I gave in the moment, an unpracticed reply to an unexpected question, was this: "Religion and urbanization are two of the world's most powerful forces, but it's also personal for me. You know, I've had life-changing experiences in and with cities. And I've always had a serious interest in ethics, but more personally, I *am* a Christian, and I'm interested in the ways in which I might think more carefully about the intersection of my own faith and my scholarship on cities and environmental politics." To this answer she raised, with an air of polite incredulity, another, more personal, question: "You're a *practicing* Christian?"

By asking whether I was a *practicing* Christian, she wanted to know whether, on the one hand, I simply grew up in a Christian home or identified in some loose fashion with the Christian tradition, or on the other hand, I actually went to church and confessed faith in Jesus Christ. After confirming that I do indeed attend church and confess faith in Jesus Christ, I began to map out for her the ways in which I personally feel called to explore connections between my Christian faith and my studies of cities and urban life.

"Good for you!" she said, and she meant it. "I think if you want to do that, you should. I'm sick and tired of asking younger scholars what they plan to do next and hearing them say that they're trying to figure out what an editor wants or what could possibly be published. No: that's just exhausting! What I like about you, Noah, is that you know just what you want to do and you do it. So if you want to do this, I think you should!" I thanked her for her support and joked that I found it refreshing that she so admired what she saw as a certain independence and determination.

This conversation is permanently etched in my memory, both because such conversations are rare and because I wish I could do it over again. What this distinguished scholar—an atheist, but not at all militantly anti-Christian—wanted was to understand the intersection of faith and learning. In a sense, her question was a contemporary twist on the church father Tertullian's famous question, "What has Athens to do with Jerusalem?"[1] Of course, Tertullian was asking about the relationship between philosophy and the Christian faith. Athens served as the symbolic geographical center of gravity for Greek philosophy, and at the time philosophy was the most influential way of thinking about almost anything. People turned to philosophy to explain the world. My interlocutor might have revised the question, though: "What has Chicago to do with Jerusalem?" And it would not have been as far off from the spirit of Tertullian's question as it appears. With so many today recognizing the waxing influence of cities in global affairs, nearly everywhere we turn, people are studying cities to explain the world. As sociologist Richard Florida writes, "Cities shape and structure our increasingly interconnected planet."[2] Or as I have argued elsewhere, "Cities make the world."[3]

So this eminent scholar was putting to me what was really a contemporary twist on a timeless question, to which I gave an all-too-timely answer. She was asking me a question that, in a sense, could be asked of any Christian, and I gave her a very personal, individual answer. She asked, "Why you?" And I gave her a very "Why me?" answer.

As I look back on it now, I wish I had responded differently. The answers I gave that day left open the possibility of an almost accidental relationship between my Christian faith and my studies of cities, as if quirkily I just happened to be interested in the intersection of the two, but it's more or less optional to make those connections. I answered as if "Yes, I am a practicing Christian and *in addition*, I am interested in the ways in which Christianity relates to what I study." My answer, you see, left open the possibility that making the connections between my studies and my faith was just another product of my autonomy, of the independence and determination that she found so commendable.

Looking back on this conversation, I sometimes wish I had emphasized less the *freedom* I feel to connect urban studies and Christian faith and emphasized more the *necessity* to do the same. I sometimes wish I had highlighted less the *idiosyncrasy* of my own interests and highlighted more a *heritage* of relating all of life to the faith. I wish I had mentioned that the command to "Love the Lord your God with all your heart and with all your soul and with all your mind" (Matthew 22:37; see also Deuteronomy 6:5) left nothing out,[4] and certainly could not exclude my work in urban studies. I wish I had mentioned the legacy of the apostle Paul, who implored the Corinthian church to "take captive *every thought* to make it obedient to Christ" (2 Corinthians 10:5, emphasis added). I wish I had underscored the rich history of Christians bringing to bear the resources of their faith on the most pressing matters of their time, such as war, slavery, and the environment. I wish I had invoked Abraham Kuyper, who said, "There is not a square inch in the whole domain of our human existence over which Christ, who is sovereign over all, does not cry, 'Mine!'"[5] But rather than Kuyper's resounding "Mine!" of the One "in [whom] all things were created" and "in [whom] all things hold together" (Colossians 1:16–17), I managed only a much more feeble "mine!"

Instead, when asked whether I was in fact a practicing Christian, I should have answered, "Yes, and *because* I'm a practicing Christian, I must connect my faith to my work as an urbanist. While practicing Christians never do less than join with other believers in confessing faith in Jesus Christ, they certainly do more, and one of the things that they do is connect their faith to all that they do and think. And that's why I'm interested in the intersection of cities, urban life, and Christian theology." As a Christian who studies cities and urban life, exploring these intersections is not optional. Christian theology is closely related to my practice of urban studies. How I study urban life and how I think about Christian doctrine must be connected. As Beth Jones writes, "Christian doctrine is intimately connected with faithful practice in the Christian life."[6] How we make those connections may differ from one person to another, but whether or not we make them isn't up for discussion.

So when Gene Green asked if I thought that the Christian tradition had anything to do with urban life, I said, "Yes." When he asked if I thought my personal experiences in cities around the world could be connected with my faith, I said, "Definitely." When he asked if my studies of urbanism could be connected with theology, I said, "Absolutely." When Gene invited me to explore that connection in this book series, I accepted, not just because I can, not just because I want to, but because I must. The question is not *whether* cities and urban life are related to theology, but *how*.

So, "What has Chicago to do with Jerusalem?" We're about to find out.

ENCOUNTERING CITIES

Taking a Closer Look at Urban Life

Mexico City, summer 1998. That was my pivotal encounter with a city, the first time I was challenged to put my faith into conversation with the complexities and realities of urban life. What I didn't know was that it was just the beginning of that work.

I had joined a study-abroad trip during the summer between my junior and senior years at Wheaton College. The program required intensive study of Spanish language along with Mexican literature and culture. Some of the time would be devoted to traveling Mexico's stunningly beautiful and culturally diverse southern states, but most of our time would be spent living with host families, enjoying field experiences, and learning together in Mexico City. Of course, I attended to my assignments and practiced my Spanish. I even learned the *Jarabe Tapatio,* better known abroad as the "Mexican Hat Dance," and the *Baile de los Machetes*, a dance that is definitely safer when you're not using machetes. But during that summer something unexpected happened. What most demanded my attention were the rhythms of urban life. What most captured my imagination was the city.

Actually, Mexico City captured my imagination before I ever set foot in it. As my flight approached the city, I could see that it sprawled across a valley between towering mountains and volcanoes. It was gigantic. The lower and closer we got—the more we lost the context of the thirty-thousand-foot perspective and the more details that came into view—the more the city seemed to stretch on forever. By the time I got out of the airport, I already felt lost.

I arrived in Mexico City two weeks before any of my classmates, and even before the professor who was leading the trip, which gave me an opportunity to explore the city on my own. My early arrival had been arranged with our professor: I had agreed to assist him with "technology and logistics" in exchange for a discount on tuition and room charges. Assisting with technology meant lugging around the one laptop shared by the group—back when laptops weighed as much as a cinderblock—and finding opportunities to dial up the one AOL account shared by everyone, which was used primarily to receive messages from the students' boyfriends and girlfriends or their anxious parents. I suppose I handled this decently until the final week of the summer, when I klutzily managed to break our professor's computer. It seems the *Baile de los Machetes* could only teach me so much coordination.

Assisting with logistics primarily consisted in helping other students get settled in and arranging field trip transportation. To do this, I needed to know where every student was staying and have at least a minimal grasp of the city's form, major landmarks, and transportation system. Thus my two-week opportunity to study the city on my own. During those weeks I explored the second largest metropolitan area in the world, a city pulsing with the rhythms of urban life and teeming with close to twenty million people.[1]

For that short time I lived with a friend of our professor in an apartment overlooking a busy avenue. I spent time on the campus of the National Autonomous University of Mexico, better known as UNAM. It was the largest university in the western hemisphere, a UNESCO World Heritage Site, and home to murals by some of Mexico's most revered artists, including Diego Rivera and David Alfaro Siqueiros. I explored public transit, squeezing onto train cars with hundreds of other people in one of the most extensive subway systems in the world. I marveled at this underground transportation system, an engineering feat that takes thousands of people who don't know each other from one end of the city to another using symbols for the stops—a fountain, a coyote, a blazing sun—so that people who can't read Spanish, or can't read at all, can still find their way around. I sat for hours in the *Zócalo*, watching the crowds in a square that has been an important public gathering place for hundreds of years, first for *Mexica* ceremonies and now for protests and other political actions. On one trip, I took a walking detour and stumbled into *Xochimilco*, the city's beautiful floating gardens, and an underutilized stadium complex, a remnant of Mexico's hosting of the summer Olympics three decades before in 1968, a season of unrest and brutality in urban areas across the world.

In that summer of 1998 I was what some who study cities and urban life might call a *flâneur*, even if a very junior one.[2] *Flâneur* is a French word meaning "stroller" or "saunterer," or even "idler," "lounger," or "loafer." As a college student away for the summer, I should probably admit to my share of idling, lounging, and loafing, but this is not the sense in which an urbanist would use the word. "Strolling" is much closer to *flânerie*, the word for the way in which a *flâneur* encounters a city. A *flâneur* is a strolling observer of city life.

I know now what I did not understand during my first summer in Mexico City: that a sort of *flânerie* is what I was up to when I took *peseros*, usually old Volkswagen Buses made to seat seven but now seemingly seating seventeen, from the subway stops into some of the city's neighborhoods or out to slums on the city's outskirts and peri-urban slums. I was a sort of *flâneur* when I visited the city's museums, enjoyed the city's food—especially from street vendors—and worshiped in different churches. And when Mexico's soccer team tied the Netherlands to advance to the second round of the World Cup, I strolled the streets with thousands of celebrating fans in an intoxicating swirl of what can only be described as *futbol* nationalism.

There are some less-than-flattering characteristics of the *flâneur*, and I should own up to them. At their best, *flâneurs* may be observant and empathic, but they are usually somewhat detached. *Flâneurs* usually have little stake in the outcomes of the urban life that they observe. If something goes wrong, the *flâneur* is often able to extricate himself from the situation, while others must endure the consequences. The *flâneur* has often been described as someone who can afford the leisure time to stroll cities, observing neighborhood and city-level dynamics with very little at risk. Aside, perhaps, from the one time I was mugged on the subway, this certainly describes my encounter with Mexico City. In the same way that I strolled the streets with celebrating crowds after the Mexico-Netherlands soccer game but was not exactly celebrating *with* them, I witnessed deprivation, poverty, suffering, and vulnerability without experiencing their depths myself.

At the same time, *flânerie* has its advantages. *Flâneurs* come to know a city by strolling about with few specific objectives, having up-close encounters with and in the city, sometimes getting lost in the details, and allowing a city to confront them with the diverse characteristics and many challenges of urban life. Being a *flâneur* doesn't mean abandoning all preconceptions in our encounters with cities—that would be impossible. Rather, it means that we don't consciously allow our preconceptions to set the agenda for our encounters with and in cities. In this way, we may find our preconceptions complicated—challenged or supported—in ways that we do not expect. When we get a closer look at urban life—when we descend from the thirty-thousand-foot view to the street level—we may even find our expectations completely overturned in surprising ways.

During my first two weeks and the two months that followed, Mexico City confronted me with many distinctive characteristics, unexpected realities, and challenges of urban life. Whether you stay for two months or two decades, a city as vast as Mexico City can force you to ask many new questions. Just like the sheer volume of other people, the challenges can be staggering. As with the height and breadth of this man-made metropolis, the wonders of urban life can be breathtaking. Like the city itself, the questions and challenges it brings are both sprawling and pulsing with life.

As a student at a Christian liberal arts college, I began—just began—to put these questions into conversation with my faith. But nothing seemed as urgent as making that connection. Since that time, I have been blessed with the opportunity to think more carefully and more expansively about those same relationships between cities, urban life, and the Christian faith. How do we reckon with basic realities of cities—their physical form and relationship to nonhuman creation, their diversity, community, wealth and poverty, and their growing influence in the world—from a Christian perspective? What does it mean to develop a more informed and committed Christian perspective on urban life? "Informed" in the sense that it goes beyond superficial impressions toward a more learned, systematic, and rigorous approach; "committed" in the sense that it is in my own voice rather than at some distance. An informed perspective reflects serious engagement with Scripture and the Christian tradition. A committed perspective means that I am not merely thinking *about* Christian commitments, but I am building upon, thinking *with or through,* Christian commitments. A committed approach is not coping with or even just reasoning about the Christian tradition—it's reasoning *from* the Christian tradition. This book is one attempt to do just that.

That said, this book isn't a systematic theological account of cities, a critical account of theological or social-science scholarship, nor a treatise on urban ministry. This book does not attempt a systematic account of the origins and implications of cities from the perspective of the Christian tradition. Such projects are valuable and important but are necessarily much longer than this short volume. Readers interested in such projects are encouraged to consult Jacques Ellul's *The Meaning of the City*; Timothy Gorringe's *A Theology of the Built Environment: Justice, Empowerment, Redemption*; Mark Gornik's *To Live in Peace: Biblical Faith and the Changing Inner City*; and Philip Sheldrake's *Spiritual City: Theology, Spirituality, and the Urban*.[3]

Also, in this book I do not offer an introduction to the most challenging urban policy issues or a critical interpretation of scholarship on cities. While I will draw upon scholarly accounts of urban life, it is not my intention to introduce readers to the fault lines of social science research into cities. As for urban ministry, what could be more important in an era in which more than half of the world's population lives in urban areas? Yet this book is meant for a broader audience than just those engaged with professional or even avocational urban ministry. Only in the broadest sense of "ministry," as a holistic and integral sense of Christian calling that might be embraced by everyone, might this book be construed as a "ministry" text.[4]

What this book does offer are reflections from a Christian perspective on a constellation of important questions raised by contemporary urban life. Each reflection begins with a story, the series of which unfolds in chronological order, beginning in the summer of 1998 and ending in the fall of 2014.

Instead of attempting to condense a comprehensive treatment of cities and urban life, I've taken a selective approach to what I understand to be some of the key issues faced by and in many cities today. The questions and issues that receive treatment here are not *only* faced by and in cities—people in suburban and rural communities face similar questions and issues—but all of them are treated here with special attention to their urban dimensions, the ways in which they are inflected by city life and experienced by city-dwellers. These reflections are by no means meant to be the last word on their topics; instead, they are meant to be more like a first word, a starting point for a more examined urban life. If the relationship between theology and urban life were presented as a legal case, this book would be an opening statement—a roadmap for the kinds of arguments that would later unfold.

This means that the book will unfold less as a single coherent deliberation on cities and more as a series of brief reflections on concerns at the core of twenty-first-century urban life. Of course, that is not to imply that the topics considered here are unrelated one to another, only that I make no attempt to package them tidily.

This selective approach also means that the book is not a treatise on all that it takes for a community to thrive, everything that matters to a flourishing urban life, or all that may please and displease God in the city. Many issues of importance to some urban communities have been left out of this book. For example, some urban communities face an epidemic of violence. As I write this book, some Chicago neighborhoods are suffering waves of violent crime and a surge in gang-and-drug-related murder. While that is important, it does not receive independent treatment here. At the same time, because the reflections I offer are loosely organized around what I understand it means to be human—to be for creation, for our neighbors, and for God—issues that do not receive independent treatment here are often related to the ones that are explored. The ways of thinking that inform the chapters of this book can inform our approach to issues that are not covered here. Violence, for example, often abdicates our responsibility to others, violates our neighbor, and shatters a sense of community, and community is one theme of chapter 4.[5]

Because of its selective approach to significant themes and issues in twenty-first-century urban life, this book leaves some work to be done by readers, and readers will do that work in very different ways. For example, readers may see connections that I would not have highlighted if I had tried to package neatly the themes and issues explored here. Indeed, readers are likely to see many issues and themes that I haven't explored, and I invite them to make connections to the ones that I do treat.

The ways in which readers make these connections will depend upon their own experiences in very different cities. This, in part, is why the book's title emphasizes not a singular "city of tomorrow" but the plural "cities of tomorrow." Whether there is such a thing as "the city," in any abstract or generic sense, is a matter of considerable debate. For the purposes of this book, I have intentionally focused our attention on the plural, on the variety of experiences of urban life that will be familiar to readers.

Nevertheless, despite the fact that these reflections are neither comprehensive *nor* representative of a singular experience of urban life, the reflections do hang together, so to speak. They hang together around the theme of what it means to be human, to be created in the image of the triune God, and to be transformed by the power of the Holy Spirit into people who increasingly resemble the second person of that triune God, Jesus Christ. The book takes one important dimension of this question of what it means to be human—that human beings are made to be for God, for others, and for creation—and asks, "What are the implications of who God made us to be for how we see our cities and urban life?"[6]

By taking this approach, I intend to build a sort of infrastructure that can guide the development of answers to the questions that crop up in urban life. The book may serve for some readers as a sort of platform on which they can continue to build their own answers to the questions, the more concrete questions, that differ from one city or neighborhood to another.

This book is intended for Christians facing questions about the riddle of urban creation care, the shape of community, the challenge of wealth and poverty, and the global influence of cities. It is meant for those whose lives and livelihoods are inextricably bound up in the flourishing of their neighborhood. It is also meant for those who live in cities and in the shadow of cities, a population that is only expected to grow in the coming decades. Indeed, it is expected to grow by tomorrow. Put this book down for just a day and the world's urban population will swell by almost 200,000 before you pick it up again.[7]

In fact, just about everyone should care about cities. The number, size, and influence of cities is now so large and growing so fast that the possibility of one sort of *flânerie*, the possibility of detached observation, is dwindling, and not only for those of us who have committed ourselves to the study of urban life. In the very near future, what happens in cities will have inevitable effects upon everyone. While the cities of tomorrow will no doubt complicate and overturn our expectations—and we should be open to that—none of us should be detached observers in our increasingly urban world.

More importantly, as we will show, "detached observation" of our world—its natural environment, our human communities—is not an option for Christians made in the image of God. We are called to more than *flânerie* in God's world. When God's people were in exile in Babylon, they were tempted not to put down roots, and understandably so. They were a captive population, having been carried off from their homeland by their conquerors. A false prophet was promising a quick return from exile, and even if he was wrong, they had God's promises of restoration. They could easily have slipped into pure resentment toward their new home—detached observation would have been an improvement. But through the prophet Jeremiah, God called them to serious engagement and long-term investment:

> This is what the Lord Almighty, the God of Israel, says to all those I carried into exile from Jerusalem to Babylon: "Build houses and settle down; plant gardens and eat what they produce. Marry and have sons and daughters; find wives for your sons and give your daughters in marriage, so that they too may

have sons and daughters. Increase in number there; do not decrease. Also, seek the peace and prosperity of the city to which I have carried you into exile. Pray to the Lord for it, because if it prospers, you too will prosper." (Jeremiah 29:4–7)

We too are called to investment and even to sacrifice for the welfare of our cities.

Most importantly, none of us are at liberty to be merely *flâneurs* in the City of God. There are no detached observers of what the author of the letter to the Hebrews describes as "the city to come" (Hebrews 13:14). One essential question, which will be taken up in the penultimate chapter of the book, is how our stake in the cities of tomorrow relates to our stake in this city to come. But before we get there, we'll need to take a closer look at urban life.

ZERO BROWNFIELDS FUTURE

Confronting the Mystery of Urban Creation Care

Thirty-one percent: It was a number that changed not only my way of thinking about cities, but my life as well. It was a number that forced me to reconsider all my assumptions about the relationship between cities and the environment. It was a number that obligated me to take up the cause of creation care just when—or better yet, where—I least expected it.

I was working in Wilmington, Delaware, with a nonprofit incubator, an institution that promoted community development by helping new organizations get started at doing good work in the city. At the same time, I was enrolled in a graduate program focused on community development and nonprofit leadership. I imagined a career singularly focused on the most pressing development challenges—education, employment, housing—in urban communities: the kinds of challenges that had left an impression on me during my time in Mexico City. These seemed to me the issues most important to thriving city neighborhoods, and I was perplexed by the attention given to other seemingly less pressing matters such as the environment. At the time I could have given a soft endorsement to something like stewardship—sure, we shouldn't just trash the environment—but I would have assumed those concerns had primarily to do with the conservation of wilderness areas. I didn't understand the few community groups whose missions related to environmental issues, and I didn't understand why the graduate program in which I had enrolled included a concentration in energy and environmental policy. Why anyone interested in a flourishing city would devote their energies to environmental challenges was a mystery to me.

It was a mystery, that is, until I learned that thirty-one percent of Wilmington's tax parcels were brownfields, sites where hazardous substances, pollution, or contamination complicates development efforts.[1] These parcels, mostly abandoned industrial sites such as factories, shipyards, and tanneries, were concentrated in neighborhoods with high poverty rates and large minority populations. A legacy of pollution contributed to health problems and limited development efforts, exacerbating the vulnerability and distress of the neighborhoods most in need of development. The best efforts at education, employment, and housing were compromised by environmental challenges. Moreover, the blight of brownfields contributed to a deficit of delightful landscapes in some neighborhoods, a problem not unfamiliar to many urban communities. Those neighborhoods suffered from a problem identified by philosopher Nicholas Wolterstorff: "The tragedy of modern urban life is not only that so many in our cities are oppressed and powerless, but also that so many have nothing surrounding them in which any human being could possibly take sensory delight."[2] Brownfields were barriers to a just, prosperous, and inclusive future for Wilmington.

Remediating brownfields can be complicated and expensive, but by the time I moved to the Chicago area, a group of Wilmington policy-makers and activists were collaborating on an initiative to clean up all of the brownfields in the city. Key constituencies in the city had come to recognize the importance of a healthy environment to a vibrant urban community and had joined together to start a project called "Wilmington's Zero Brownfields Future," an effort to remediate every brownfield site in every neighborhood in the city.

Like Wilmington, most cities defy our sometimes facile assumptions about the relationship between cities and the environment, assumptions based as much upon misunderstandings of "the environment" as they are upon misunderstandings of "the city." The relationship between the two is more expansive and complicated than the brownfields problem alone can suggest. Cities are chock-full of nature, and the wilderness or rural areas that we sometimes presume are beyond the reach of urban influence have often been shaped by urban life in nearby cities. As William Cronon has pointed out, the development of Chicago may have had the greatest impact on the landscape from the Great Lakes to the Rocky Mountains, shaping the plains and upper Midwest as we know them.[3] This relationship has now taken on global dimensions as cities, which account for approximately 80 percent of human-produced greenhouse gas emissions, now shape even the world's least apparently urban landscapes by concentrating climate-disrupting activities.[4] At the same time, some cities are harnessing their potential to contribute to environmental stability and integrity, joining an emerging and potentially powerful movement or network of "green cities," a theme that has been an influential strand of urban planning since at least the 1898 publication of Ebenezer Howard's *Garden Cities of To-Morrow.*[5]

As Christians, how should we think about the relationship between cities and the environment? How should we think about the possibility of green cities? What does the Christian tradition mean for our interactions with brownfields? How does a Christian understanding of what it means to be human affect the ways in which we think about the mystery of urban creation care?

The beginning of our answer is at the beginning of the Bible. The opening chapters of Genesis portray human beings as those who are to be for the nonhuman created order. After God forms and fills his creation, he creates humans to serve as stewards and guardians of his handiwork and as images or representations of the kind of God who made and rules the universe. As Genesis 1:28 reads, "God blessed them and said to them, 'Be fruitful and increase in number; fill the earth and subdue it. Rule over the fish in the sea and the birds in the sky and over every living creature that moves on the ground.'" What does it mean to fill the earth and subdue it? Was God giving humans a license, or even a mandate, to abuse or neglect creation, to "show it who's boss?" Not at all! Genesis 2:15 helps us to understand the richer meanings of our relations with creation: "The Lord God took the man and put him in the Garden of Eden to work it and take care of it." Fill, subdue, work, take care. Daniel Block convincingly argues that these blessings and instructions entail a command to serve and to guard creation.[6] Human beings are to be a blessing to the rest of creation. We are to promote the flourishing of creation.

If Block is right, then the call to serve and to guard creation is a telling aspect of what it means to be human. Part of our calling, as images of the Creator, as his representatives, as signs that the one God is the creator and sustainer of all creation, is to care for the earth. The ways in which we live out our callings should be consonant with this mandate. When it comes to urban life, the cities we build should be places where creation flourishes and should contribute to the flourishing of creation beyond their bounds.

But Genesis 3 complicates our understanding of this calling. In it we learn that human sin has led to estrangement from nature. Following the distorting voice of the serpent, Eve and Adam neglect the word of God and eat of the only tree that had been prohibited. Because of their sin, God pronounces a curse, speaking first to the serpent, then to Eve, and then to Adam. In verses 17–19 of Genesis 3, God says to Adam,

> "Because you listened to your wife and ate fruit from the tree
> about which I commanded you, 'You must not eat from it,'

"Cursed is the ground because of you;
    through painful toil you will eat food from it
    all the days of your life.
It will produce thorns and thistles for you,
    and you will eat the plants of the field.
By the sweat of your brow
    you will eat your food
until you return to the ground,
    since from it you were taken;
for dust you are
    and to dust you will return."

The curse makes clear that the triumphs of human life will always be marked by challenge, limitation, and frustration,[7] a theme picked up by the apostle Paul in Romans 8:20–21 when he writes that the "the creation was subjected to frustration" and "bondage to decay." The acts of self-assertion recounted in the opening chapters of Genesis—human beings acting for themselves rather than for God, for each other, and for creation—plunged the nonhuman created order into bondage. As Richard Bauckham writes,

> The purpose for which God put Adam and Eve in the garden was "to till it and to keep it"; or "to cultivate and to care for it"; or "to work it and protect it" (2:15). In the garden, the combination was not a problem.[8] But after Eden, how do we both cultivate and protect nature? Evan Eisenberg suggests that this command to Adam can now be seen "as a . . . kind of riddle that we urgently need to solve. How do we protect nature from our work, and so keep from fouling the source of our own life? And how do we work with nature in a way that leaves both nature and human nature undiminished?"[9]

From the curse onward, human beings must live out, and live into, this riddle. This riddle is the context in which we build and maintain our urban communities, in which we live with the productive capacities of industrial sites and also the legacies of their pollution. This riddle is the context in which we live with the triumph of cities that have the potential to make our world a greener place[10] and the tragedy of cities that often have ill effects on the global environment.

How should we respond to the riddle of urban creation care? What resources do we draw upon? It is important to note that we have guidance, power, and hope in the face of this riddle—guidance for the ways in which we should act in the face of environmental challenges, power to act that way, and hope even when we fall short.

Guidance: Scripture teaches us that we ought to act in ways that demonstrate we are for creation, that our calling is to keep and to serve it. While Scripture does not teach us exactly what this requires in twenty-first-century cities, we should work toward urban communities that are consistent with this calling. We ought to develop neighborhoods that signify and symbolize the reconciliation of God, humanity, and nature, and not only the estrangement between them. We must stretch and sacrifice and strive to live in ways that do not burden vulnerable ecosystems, far-off communities, and future generations.

Power: The Holy Spirit illuminates God's Word and empowers us to act consistently with our calling. Because of our union with Jesus Christ, the Spirit of God is upon us, emboldening and enabling us to use our gifts on behalf of others, even when it is difficult to do so. The Spirit renews us, makes us part of the new creation, and helps us to fulfill our calling to be for creation, for God, and for others.

Hope: But what about the times when we look around and see the yawning gap between a creation burdened by frustration and the new creation, set free to be what God intended? What about the times when we ourselves fall short? When we cannot or do not do what we ought to do with regard to cities and the environment? In that case, we have hope in a God who will one day restore all things to their rightful order. This work is most perfectly demonstrated in the resurrection of Jesus Christ, whose body was rescued from decay and raised in perfection. One day, the same power that raised Jesus Christ from the dead will consummate a work of new creation more expansive than we can possibly imagine. The work he has already begun by the power of the Holy Spirit will be fulfilled on the last day. The apostle Paul writes in Romans 8:18–22,

> I consider that our present sufferings are not worth comparing with the glory that will be revealed in us. For the creation waits in eager expectation for the children of God to be revealed. For the creation was subjected to frustration, not by its own choice, but by the will of the one who subjected it, in hope that the creation itself will be liberated from its bondage to decay and brought into the freedom and glory of the children of God.

To give creation a taste of this liberation, a taste of freedom, is to give it a brief glimpse of us as the children of God, as his images, as representations of what he is like. It is, in other words, to be the human beings that he made us to be. But one day God will replace brief glimpses and little tastes with a transformation beyond our imagination. While creation has been in bondage to decay since the fall and the curse, while we continue to see evidence of futility and frustration, while we are surrounded by evidence that we are unable to solve the riddle of creation care in any permanent fashion, at the same time we know that God will set it right one day. The day of the Lord is the day in which he will deliver us, just as he brought his people out of Egypt and into a promised land filled with vineyards and cities that they did not build with their own hands (Joshua 24:13; see also Deuteronomy 6:10), into an everlasting garden city that we did not build with our own hands.

What is the upshot for urban life? Our cities are concrete examples of the enduring riddle of creation care—they are evidence of our filling and subduing, but they constantly demand that we attend to questions of serving and keeping. We should inhabit our cities—and God's world—in a way that shows that we embrace our calling to live into that riddle, that we have guidance, power, and hope in the face of that riddle. Cleaning up brownfields, providing and maintaining green space, ensuring access to delightful landscapes, and reducing our burdens on vulnerable communities and future generations are all important tasks for our urban life. Cities give us opportunities to "live smaller, live closer together, and drive less,"[11] and to the extent that all three are good for the environment, from the neighborhood level to the global scale, perhaps Christians should be leading on these things. We are empowered by the Holy Spirit to put creation and others first as we undertake these tasks.

But our efforts will sometimes fall short. Though Wilmington, for example, has made progress on brownfield remediation, it hasn't exactly achieved the "Zero Brownfields Future" that so many have hoped for and worked toward. We should meet such failures with lament, not blithe acceptance. But our lament should be coupled with hope. When we do fall short, we can remind ourselves that God, beginning with Jesus Christ, has already begun the work of the new creation and promises one day to bring us into a city where not only are there no tears, but there are also no brownfields: a truly "Zero Brownfields Future."

THE SHAPE OF COMMUNITY

Living with Other People in Cities

In the past eight years, I've spent a lot of time in Uptown, a neighborhood on Chicago's north side, where I direct a semester-long experiential, residential program of urban studies. Students in the program spend sixteen weeks studying, living in, learning from, and working for the good of Chicago. They live together in three apartments, take upper-level courses in urban studies and theology, and intern with some of the most innovative organizations in the city. Through the program, students discern the shape of community—the way of living with others who are not like us—both within and beyond their student cohort.

When I began this work in the fall of 2006, I didn't have an office in our Uptown building. So I searched for an appropriate space for regular meetings with our students. Libraries were sparse and full of patrons who might not appreciate overhearing hours of our conversations. Restaurants, on the other hand, were abundant, and their customers would probably find our conversations minimally disruptive. And what better way to discuss what students are learning than over a meal? So, after a bit of dining around, I settled on Alma Pita, a small Mediterranean restaurant on Wilson Avenue, one of Uptown's main thoroughfares.

Stretching west from Lakeshore Drive, the Wilson Avenue

corridor bustled with all kinds of activity. Harry S. Truman College, with more than 23,000 students from over 150 countries, sat across the street from Alma Pita. To the west was the American Indian Center, an institute fostering the welfare of Indian people of all tribes in the Chicago area and promoting "bonds of understanding and communication" between Indians and non-Indians in the city. Just a block away was a busy stop on the Red Line of Chicago's elevated train system, the "El," and an innovative social-service organization that served the local homeless population. Occasional outbursts of gang violence would visit several of the corners to the east. And in the short stroll to the lakefront, I would pass fixtures of Christian service in the neighborhood: Uptown Baptist Church and Emmaus Ministries, a ministry to homosexual male prostitutes in the neighborhood. Alma Pita was in the middle of it all.

For most of six years, I ate dinner at Alma Pita once a week, treating students to free hummus and falafel if they joined me there for discussions of what they were learning in class, at their internship sites, in their service placements, or through their temporary but very intentional community of like-minded classmates. Our program was intended to be a stretching and transformative experience, and I wanted to know how that process of transformation was going. Moreover, it is precisely the process of regular reflection that so often lends such experiences life-changing potential.

Alma Pita was a fixture in the community, always busy during lunch and dinner, with a steady stream of dine-in and take-out customers who knew the owners well. We too got to know the owners. So it was a sad day when, six years later, Alma Pita closed. Still, I had to decide on a new place to host students for meetings and dinner. Within just a few blocks, I had an incredible variety of options, beginning with local coffee shops (it isn't only the students who need caffeine before class!) and including Ethiopian, Ghanaian, Korean, Mexican, and Thai restaurants.

To those familiar with Uptown, this would not come as a

surprise. Indeed, one of the few things more amazing than Uptown's culinary diversity is the ethnic diversity of the neighborhood's residents. Uptown is one of Chicago's most diverse neighborhoods. Once a ritzy northside neighborhood with the city's liveliest arts scene, the community has a rich history as a destination for migrant populations from around Chicago, the metro area, the United States, and the world. The neighborhood became extraordinarily diverse after World War II, when "whites from Appalachia, Japanese Americans from California, and Native Americans from Wisconsin, Minnesota, and Oklahoma settled in Uptown's affordable but deteriorating housing.[1] In addition, the state of Illinois channeled released mental health patients to Uptown's small apartments and halfway houses."[2] Recent developments— including both global dynamics and neighborhood-level policy decisions[3]—have also contributed to Uptown's distinctive diversity. Because of an influx of immigrants, Uptown is the site of Chicago's "New Chinatown" and what some have called the "quintessential Little Vietnam." In the past few decades, many neighborhood-level authorities have been intentional about requiring all new housing developments to include a greater than usual number of affordable housing units, thus ensuring a basic level of socioeconomic diversity, which in the United States too often correlates with race and ethnicity. In its extraordinary diversity, Uptown is a microcosm of Chicago, which is one of the most diverse cities in the world.

Even though only a handful of cities can boast anything like Chicago's diversity, racial and ethnic relations have been a—perhaps *the*—defining issue faced by cities in the United States. East Coast and Midwest cities were "arrival cities"—destinations for many of the world's poorest migrant populations from the eighteenth to the twentieth centuries—well before we knew the term.[4] From the Civil War to World War II, the massive growth of urban areas in the northern United States was fueled in part by three great migrations of blacks from the South who fled a landscape of slavery and persecution but encountered new, powerful, and very active forms of discrimination in the North.[5] Finally, the second half of the twentieth century saw a massive boom in immigration from Latin America that has reshaped U.S. cities from coast to coast.

While racial and ethnic diversity are not always and everywhere defining features of urban life—it is important to understand that cities in many parts of the world have been relatively homogenous compared to those in the United States—it remains a key issue of urban life. For example, in his history of Cairo, Nezar Al Sayyad shows that the Egyptian capitol has had many ethnic enclaves, more or less voluntary communities consisting of one ethnic group, for centuries. Some cities, like Shanghai, were built as intentionally cosmopolitan centers.[6] And contemporary global dynamics have made many cities more diverse as developments in transportation and communication technologies make it easier for people to relocate.[7] From the "high-end globalization" of advanced producer and financial services, such as accounting and management consulting, to the "low-end globalization" of trade in used cellular phones and other electronics, economic interconnections continue to bring people together in our cities. In his book *Ghetto at the Center of the World*, Gordon Mathews highlights a *single building* in Hong Kong that houses a diversity of people representing 129 nationalities and a multitude of religions.[8] Housing people from all over the world who come to make a living by trading relatively inexpensive goods and services, Chungking Mansions represents the sort of urbanism that we see more and more of every day. Indeed, Mathews sees in Chungking Mansions a picture of the cities of tomorrow.

What effects does this diversity-in-community have today? Will increasingly diverse communities be a blessing or a curse to the cities of tomorrow?

Behind these questions lies a raging debate about what happens when so many different people come together in the city. Many think that the proximity of different groups will cause the emergence of new forms of racism, radicalism, and fundamentalism, perhaps even reinforcing patterns of worldwide violence, especially where religious difference is concerned.[9] Indeed, for decades, many sociologists believed that cities would undermine the social fabric as new and diverse social forms dramatically reordered, replaced, and destabilized existing social forms.[10] Others, however, expect a future in which living together in our diverse cities leads to a future of cosmopolitan coexistence. Some of the greatest urbanists of the twentieth century, including Jane Jacobs and Lewis Mumford, emphasized diversity as one of the hallmarks of a thriving city and the key to a vibrant urban future.[11] And in Chungking Mansions, Mathews finds people with very different national origins, ethnic backgrounds, and religious commitments not only peacefully coexisting, but depending upon each other to flourish.

But Chungking Mansions and Uptown reveal something far more basic, far more fundamental, than racial, ethnic, religious, and socioeconomic diversity. They reveal that the city is full of what we might bluntly call "other people." Sure, the city is full of people of various races and ethnicities. It is full of people of various religious backgrounds. It is full of people with varying socioeconomic backgrounds. It is full of people from around the world. It is marked by diversities inflected by layer upon layer of power and, often, structural discrimination and exploitation. But without diminishing the importance of historically power-inflected and sometimes exploitative relationships between races, ethnic groups, and classes, it is safe to say that the most basic form of diversity that Uptown and Chungking Mansions share with every other city in the world is actually the simple diversity of encountering many other people who are different from us.

This can be one of the most striking characteristics of urban life: the city is full of other people, each one different from another! There is an important sense in which this is why cities exist. In a very basic sense, cities are concentrations or agglomerations of many people, each different from the others and all taking advantage of what we call "propinquity" or the state of being close to someone or something else, a state that reaches a certain density in urban areas. This propinquity creates both economic and cultural dynamism, thus attracting more people. It is both a consequence and a cause of the growth of cities, evidence of a positive feedback loop, or results that reinforce their causes. Cities attract people, grow larger, and attract more people. Indeed, as William H. Whyte notes in his classic study of urban places, "What attracts people most, it would appear, is other people."[12]

It is no wonder, then, that many of our most challenging questions about the city have to do with questions of difference, questions that other people put to us more sharply than any other experience in our lives. What should we make of this as Christians? How do Scripture and the Christian tradition speak to the way we should live with other people who are very different from us? Is there a "Christian shape" to community? What does the sociological reality of diversity in community have to do with the theological reality of being made in the image of God? How and where do we learn to live out the shape of community?

Just as we suggested in the previous chapter on the riddle of urban creation care, the question of how we should relate to the diversity of other human beings in the city is one that touches on what it means for us to be human. And as we suggested above, we should start in the beginning.

To say, as Genesis does and the rest of Scripture affirms, that we are made in the image of God is to say that we, like the Trinity, have our being in and through relationships with others. In his explanation of Karl Barth's theological anthropology, Wolf Krötke explains that the sociological reality of human relationships is related to the theological reality of being made in the image of God: "It is no accident that the human creature exists structurally in relations.

Rather, this relationality must be understood as an external expression of the fact that the triune God himself exists as Father, Son, and Spirit in relations, namely in the relation of love."[13] What this means is that we are made like the Trinity. When God said, "Let us make mankind in our image, in our likeness" (Genesis 1:26), this meant, let us make a creature that exists in relationships that mirror those of the triune God. God has existed from before all time in a relationship that the church has described as *perichoresis*, in which each person of the Trinity dwells with, in, and for the others. And just as the Trinity consists of three persons, each irreducible and not to be confused with the others and yet all in a perfect community of love, all of us as individuals are made to be in community with others who are different from us.

God made us to be, like the Trinity, in relations of love with one another, to be in, with, and for others. This is the reason that God, as recounted in Genesis 2:18, judges that it is "not good for the man to be alone," taking part of Adam to make Eve and creating a relationship in which each lives for the other. This is the reason that Leviticus 19:18 instructs God's people to love their neighbors as themselves. This is the reason that Jesus, when asked what the greatest commandment is, answers, "'Love the Lord your God with all your heart and with all your soul and with all your mind.' This is the first and greatest commandment. And the second is like it: 'Love your neighbor as yourself'" (Matthew 22:37–39). Perhaps more to the point, this is the reason that Jesus added, "All the Law and the Prophets hang on these two commandments" (Matthew 22:40). All the Law and the Prophets hang on these two commandments because all the Law and the Prophets teach us how to be the images of God that we were intended to be. Commandments to love one another teach us to be truly human, and to be truly human is to exist in relationships of love.

Just as there is an estrangement between human beings and nonhuman creation, however, there is also estrangement between human beings and other human beings. This relationship of each one being for and in the others is perverted with the acts of self-assertion represented by the fall. In the curse, God pronounces that Eve and Adam will have their proper desire to serve the other disordered, bent into a desire to lord it over the other. Yet even the curse, by describing the ways in which normative relations with other human beings have been perverted and go wrong, brings a certain forceful clarity to the ways in which we ought to relate to others if we are to get things right.

Of course, Jesus Christ, the perfect image of God, comes both to reverse the curse and to teach us what it means to be truly human. As Paul writes in Philippians 2:5–8,

> In your relationships with one another, have the same mindset as Christ Jesus: Who, being in very nature God, did not consider equality with God something to be used to his own advantage; rather, he made himself nothing by taking the very nature of a servant, being made in human likeness. And being found in appearance as a man, he humbled himself by becoming obedient to death—even death on a cross!

Through Jesus' perfect work of being for others, God reconciles us to himself by atoning for our sins *and* shows us what it means to be human, and he did it despite the great differences and alienation that had come between us and God. As Paul says, "God demonstrates his own love for us in this: While we were still sinners, Christ died for us" (Romans 5:8).

Jesus' perfection in being for others is vindicated by his resurrection in the power of the Holy Spirit, and because of our union with Jesus Christ, this same Holy Spirit raises us from the deadness of our self-assertion and empowers us to be for others as well. The Holy Spirit not only gives us gifts but also teaches and empowers us to use those gifts in the service of others. This is the essence of new creation—that we would be transformed into people who would perfectly be for others, who would perfectly love our neighbors as ourselves, who would perfectly reflect God's own being-for-others, and who, by doing so, would perfectly express our being-for-God.

This teaching that we were made for community in diversity is important to how we understand urban life. First, there is a descriptive dimension of this doctrine that is basic to our understanding of community in diversity. We should recognize that we have our identity in community and relationship—this is a fact, not only a norm. We are not simply what we make of ourselves. Rather, we are made by our life together with others. This recognition cuts against the grain of so much that we otherwise learn about who we are and how our identities are constituted.

The descriptive aspect of this teaching suggests that community is not a matter of choice. It is not a question of whether we want to embrace our being in relationship with others. We simply *are* in relationship with others. We cannot opt out. The fact that we cannot opt out of relationship, but exist in permanent, irreducible, nonnegotiable relationship with others, also means that any attempt to opt out of relationship and community is actually just one way to be in relationship, one mode of being in community, and it's often a damaging one. This means that when we are surrounded by so many people so different from us, when millions of other people in our cities share a common fate, we literally cannot—I don't mean "must not"—opt out of being in relationship with those people. Community is not a catchphrase to be bandied about in reference to relationships we want or choose. We are not only in relationship with others like us, nor are we only in relationship with others we like. Community is a fact, not a slogan.

If we cannot opt out of community, then the question is *how,* not whether, we should be in community. Being images of the triune God has implications for how we live out these relationships. The indicative has a clear imperative. We should, as Scripture teaches us, be for others. One thing this teaching suggests about urban life is that we should not only tolerate the things that make us different; we should also celebrate them and find in and through diversity opportunities to serve our neighbor—our neighbor who is very different from us. We are to love our neighbors, to help our neighbors flourish, no matter how different we are from them.

Even if someone is different from us in embracing this call to love others, even if they don't love us, we are to love them. We are to seek their thriving, even if they do not seek ours. As Jesus says in the Sermon on the Mount,

> You have heard that it was said, 'Love your neighbor and hate your enemy.' But I tell you, love your enemies and pray for those who persecute you, that you may be children of your Father in heaven. He causes his sun to rise on the evil and the good, and sends rain on the righteous and the unrighteous. If you love those who love you, what reward will you get? Are not even the tax collectors doing that? And if you greet only your own people, what are you doing more than others? Do not even pagans do that? Be perfect, therefore, as your heavenly Father is perfect. (Matthew 5:43–48)

Jesus points out that even tax collectors—considered traitors to their own religion and ethnicity—loved those who loved them. Even those people who do not belong to God treat with respect those who are like them. So what sets God's people apart? Loving those who are different. And why should they do it? To be perfect as their heavenly Father is perfect. Again, the sense in which we should be for others is linked closely to the sense in which we are to be like God, to be his images, representations of his perfect kindness.

But this imperative to love others by being for them and seeking their good must not be abused. On one extreme, we may sometimes face the temptation to use this teaching as a license for exploitation.

Noting that each person is called to serve others can be perverted to force others to serve us. This teaching can be used as a way to legitimate status quo power relationships in which one group of people is exploiting another in ways that undermine Scripture's entire teaching on community in diversity. The realities of community in diversity are not a license to tell the vulnerable that their lot is to serve the powerful.

On the other hand, we sometimes face a powerful but opposite temptation: to apply this insight only to our own lives, to remind ourselves that we should be serving and living in and for others while taking care not to force our neighbors to live in and for others themselves. This too is dangerous. As much as we must apply this teaching to ourselves, limiting its application in that way can rob our teaching of its prophetic power. We must be able to call our neighbors into lives lived in love for others. Here we find theological resources for understanding and negotiating the community in diversity that is urban life. We learn that community in diversity is an unavoidable fact, but that *loving* community in diversity is the goal or standard to which all are called.

While our calling to love others is not limited to our brothers and sisters in Christ, the church is one place we should witness this loving community in diversity and learn how to live it out. In fact, the apostle Paul indicates that the church *is* God's new creation for this reason: It is the place where differences don't keep us apart, where "there is no Gentile or Jew, circumcised or uncircumcised, barbarian, Scythian, slave or free, but Christ is all, and is in all" (Colossians 3:11; see also Galatians 3:28), but rather, it is the place where differences are celebrated. It is a place where a diversity of gifts and roles, ethnicities and social statuses, are characterized by community in the Spirit. As Paul writes to the church in Corinth (1 Corinthians 12:4–11), God's people are given many different kinds of gifts but are unified despite these differences by the one God who gives and governs them. Paul then goes on in verse 12 to liken our unity in the church to united parts of one body in which each member is important: "Just as a body, though one, has many parts, but all its many parts form one body, so it is with Christ."

In likening the Christian community to the body, Paul drew upon, but also subverted, an image often used in the ancient world to promote social and political unity. As Margaret Mitchell points out, Paul's metaphor of the body paralleled language often used "as an appeal for concord in Greco-Roman antiquity."[14] While the body metaphor was often used in the ancient world to reinforce unity in diversity, however, it also emphasized that those of lower social status needed those of higher social status, that the lesser parts of the body needed the greater parts. Paul turns this impulse on its head. While he does not make a revolutionary claim that differences in social status must be abolished, he does write that no part of the body may insist that other parts do not belong, and even "the head cannot say to the feet, 'I don't need you!" (1 Corinthians 12:21). The most vulnerable parts are yet indispensable, the lesser parts are yet treated with honor, and all parts "should have equal concern for each other" (1 Corinthians 12:22–25). And lest we think that Paul's "body-talk" has to do only with spiritual gifts, in 1 Corinthians 12:13, he makes clear that this applies to ethnicity and social status: "For we were all baptized by one Spirit so as to form one body— whether Jews or Gentiles, slave or free—and we were all given the one Spirit to drink."

God's intention for his people to exhibit community in diversity represents his ultimate intention for the new creation. In Ephesians, Paul reveals God's plan "to bring unity to all things in heaven and on earth under Christ" (1:10), a unity that brings together Jew and Gentile, not by collapsing distinctions between the two but by destroying "the barrier, the dividing wall of hostility" (2:14). This work of unification is accomplished "by the blood of Christ" (2:13) and "through the cross" (2:16). Here we encounter the shape of community. It is through the sacrifice of Jesus Christ that God has created one new humanity. Through Jesus Christ we learn that the shape of community is the cross.

We must learn to live into the cruciform shape of community—that is, we should live out community in ways that are shaped by and like the cross. We must hope for neighborhoods marked by harmony in the midst of racial, ethnic, religious, and other sorts of diversity. We must work toward cities in which people who are very different may thrive. This means addressing structures of discrimination and oppression and creating conditions in which all may flourish.

The church must be a place where this is lived out and modeled. A stroll through Uptown is enough to remind us of the sociological reality of diversity in community, but we must have practices that teach us the theological reality of the loving relationships of service and justice that should bind us together.

As I write these words, I am preparing for a service experience with some of our newest students—freshman and transfers who have chosen to begin their Wheaton College experience with a week of service in Chicago. On just their fourth day at Wheaton College, these students will be joining a ministry in the city that teaches churches to accept, celebrate, and love others who are not like themselves. The Bridge at Mission: USA is a ministry that involves local churches in serving a population of recovering addicts, prostitutes, and primarily prison inmates recently released into the local community. Local churches and others help by providing meals and assisting with a weekly worship service.

On the surface, it appears that these local churches are serving ex-inmates, often new disciples of Christ, in their transformation, in leaving behind ungodly choices, in putting off the old self and putting on the new (Ephesians 4:24, Colossians 3:10). But the genius of this ministry is the way in which it teaches churches how to be God's new creation. The fact is that many addicts, prostitutes, and people recently released from prison come to faith in Jesus Christ and want to worship with his people. But when they show up at church, they are often treated as if, because of their differences, they don't belong. They attend church and—because they look different, speak differently, act differently—they worship amid glares and questions about whether or not they belong. The cold shoulder would be an improvement over some of the receptions they've experienced. Churches that don't receive these brothers and sisters in Christ with hospitality are grieving the one Holy Spirit who unites all of us with each other in a new creation that is a fact, whether or not we choose it or always live up to it.

By involving churches in their ministry, The Bridge isn't just teaching recovering addicts, prostitutes, and ex-inmates to put on the new man by putting bad choices behind them. It is also teaching local churches and others in the Chicago area to put on their new selves—to embrace unity in diversity—by embracing others despite their differences. Through this practice, God is teaching my students and me how to live in diverse communities like Uptown. He is revealing us to be part of his people, his one humanity, the new creation. He is empowering us to be truly human. As we minister together under the cross, God is teaching us the shape of community.

CARING FOR THE LEAST OF THESE

Responding to Vulnerability in Cities

It was a chill morning in Detroit—a cool but clear day for the annual Thanksgiving Day Parade. It's called America's Thanksgiving Parade, and it's been going on since Detroit was America's City, since it was one of the wealthiest and most economically productive cities in the world. My family and I set up on the corner of Woodward and Stimson, just half a block from the headquarters of the Detroit Rescue Mission Ministries, one of the largest homeless shelters in the country. Though the Rescue Mission has been open for more than a century, it has never been busier than now. Along with most of southeastern Michigan, Detroit plunged into a recession well before the rest of the country did in 2008. Then, after decades of severe economic pressure, just when it seemed things couldn't get worse, they did. While pockets of the Detroit area still enjoy the wealth that marked the city's heyday, large swaths of the city have experienced one of the most complicated and seemingly intractable urban economic calamities of our times. The once proud city is now probably the most infamous site for what is commonly called "ruin porn"—vivid photographic and video displays of material decline.

The parade included a number of standards: floats, local politicians, a brigade of clever men clad in business attire and spinning briefcases the way that majorettes twirl batons. The procession also included the usual glitz: a local celebrity who had made it big on *American Idol* and a couple of extravagant floats sponsored by the down-but-not-out Michigan-based auto manufacturers. But it also includes some Detroit distinctives—a large number of *papier-mâché* heads and a huge balloon of Captain Underpants. The giant *papier-mâché* heads, worn by parade-participants-turned-bobble-head-dolls, seem to be refreshed every year. Captain Underpants was a different story.

As Captain Underpants approached our corner, it was clear that he was none too steady, that the dozen or so handlers with wires, walking underneath him, had their work cut out for them. But when they drew closer, the crowd started chanting, "Spin it! Spin it! Spin it!"—a staple of the Detroit parade is for the crowd to demand that the handlers spin the balloons. When the handlers did spin the balloon, it became apparent that Captain Underpants, like the city, had seen better days. What little clothing he wore was quite tattered. From his cape to his briefs, Captain Underpants' wardrobe was in some distress. But he made it to the end of the parade despite the tattered look.

After the parade, as we passed down the block, heading toward the Mission, we noticed that the block, like Captain Underpants, was also tattered. Broken windows, abandoned lots, vacant buildings. All signs of the poverty and distress that have marked this city for years. Across Woodward from where we had taken in the parade, many watched from the local Starbucks, sheltered from the elements with warm five-dollar beverages in hand, while behind and around us on Stimson, many hung over the balconies of their dilapidated public housing units. Later that day, after the parade, the Detroit Rescue Mission would serve almost five thousand Thanksgiving meals to Detroit's homeless and otherwise vulnerable populations.

Detroit is not alone. While many of our cities are home to some of the world's wealthiest communities, many are also home to some of the most impoverished, distressed, and vulnerable. We now live in a world that Mike Davis refers to as a "planet of slums."[1] Slums built on garbage heaps in Guatemala City and Manila. And from Mumbai to Rio de Janeiro to Nairobi, there are now slums with more than one million residents—bigger than most cities before the twentieth century.

Let that sink in for just a minute.

Each of these slums houses a population more than 40 percent larger than that of Detroit.

Vulnerability and distress are not limited to our biggest cities but are characteristic of our suburbs too. In fact, in much of the world it is the suburbs and not the centers of cities that are characterized by poverty, vulnerability, and distress. And in the United States, poverty is growing fastest at the edges of our most populated metropolitan areas.

So it was no surprise when the plight of the poor was a topic of discussion at a recent planning meeting for a suburban municipality that intended to develop a "Tax Increment Financing," or TIF, district to raise money for economic development efforts. A TIF district allows revenues raised through taxes to be folded back into development efforts in the district. Once a TIF district is established, all new net taxes from that area can only be used to improve that district in ways that are likely to advance the cause of economic development. TIF districts are complicated instruments. They can do a lot of good. They can also cause a lot of harm. They are, for example, known to compromise the stability of affordable housing units in and around the district as property values increase due to public and private investment. And while residents inside the district are afforded a number of protections and concessions, such as assistance with the costs of relocation in the case of possible displacement, residents outside, even *just* outside, the district's boundaries are afforded no additional protections or concessions if they are displaced.

The meeting I attended was prompted by the concerns of a community that had made their homes in subsidized housing units at the edge of the proposed TIF district. The plans threatened the possible displacement of a large community of immigrants, most of whom were poor and many of whom were refugees and had previously been targets of political and religious persecution. I had attended the meeting in order to join with others in speaking on behalf of that community.

When the meeting started, I had to submit a form declaring my intention to speak. When I submitted the form, I didn't know what I would say when my turn came. Luckily, planning meetings—especially contentious ones—often move very slowly, so I had time to peruse my Bible and make a few notes. What does it mean, I wondered, to be truly human—to be the images of God that we were meant to be—when it comes to our response to poverty and other forms of vulnerability?

As I prepared for my remarks, I was drawn to the Book of Daniel, specifically the "Nebuchadnezzar Cycle" of stories in chapters 2–4. We can easily miss the big picture of these chapters when we read them one at a time as we usually do. But if we read them together, we get a picture of what it should mean to be like God and what it should mean to be fully human. And there's a perhaps surprising message about caring for the poor. It's a message I shared with the people at this planning meeting.

In Daniel 2 we encounter Nebuchadnezzar, raving mad after a troubling dream. He insists that someone among his many wise men—his magicians, enchanters, and sorcerers—must tell him not only what the dream means, but also what the dream *was*. That is, he has no plans to tell them the dream so that they can interpret it. Rather, he is measuring their expertise and authority in the interpretation by whether or not they actually need to know the dream in advance. A truly reliable interpreter, he seems to think, doesn't need to be told what the dream was. At first it doesn't seem that anyone will live up to his expectations. Indeed, his wise men tell him that he is asking for something humanly impossible: "The thing that the king is asking is too difficult, and no one can reveal it to the king except the gods, whose dwelling is not with mortals" (Daniel 2:11 NRSV).

Just as Nebuchadnezzar is about to kill his wise men—to tear them limb from limb and leave their houses in ruins—for their failure both to tell and to interpret his dream, God gives Daniel both the content and the interpretation of the dream: Nebuchadnezzar dreamt of a statue of five different materials and of a stone not cut by human hands that destroys the statue and becomes a great mountain, filling the whole earth. Daniel tells Nebuchadnezzar that the statue represents a timeline of sorts, with successive kingdoms represented by different materials, and his kingdom is represented by the statue's head of gold. The rock that rolls out of the mountainside is the rock that will destroy the statue—it represents the kingdom not made by human hands that will overthrow all human kingdoms: "In the days of those kings the God of heaven will set up a kingdom that shall never be destroyed, nor shall this kingdom be left to another people. It shall crush all these kingdoms and bring them to an end, and it shall stand forever; just as you saw that a stone was cut from the mountain not by hands, and that it crushed the iron, the bronze, the clay, the silver, and the gold" (Daniel 2:44–45 NRSV).

Nebuchadnezzar was apparently ambivalent about this interpretation: on the one hand, he rewarded Daniel for telling and interpreting the dream, giving him gifts, putting him in charge of the province of Babylon, and setting him over all of the other wise men; on the other hand, Nebuchadnezzar apparently didn't like the idea that his kingdom might not last forever. The very next thing recounted in the book of Daniel is Nebuchadnezzar's making a statue of all gold and insisting that everyone in his kingdom bow down to worship it. Here's one of the connections we miss when we read these stories separately, or when we read them as if the point of chapter 3 is the heroic faith of Daniel's three friends. By making a statue that is gold from head to toe, Nebuchadnezzar was saying, "If the statue is a timeline, and if my kingdom is represented by gold, then the golden part should be from head to toe! My kingdom is forever. No other kingdom will come after it. No otherworldly 'rock uncut by human hands' will roll out of a mountainside and destroy it. Bow down and worship *my* eternal kingdom!" We might miss the point, but Shadrach, Meshach, and Abednego didn't. By refusing to bow down and declare their allegiance to Nebuchadnezzar's supposedly eternal kingdom, they were declaring again their allegiance to the one true God whose kingdom is forever. For this they were bound and thrown into a fiery furnace, where they were joined and protected by a powerful otherworldly figure of the sort that Nebuchadnezzar was insisting could not thwart his intentions.

In chapter 4, we learn that Nebuchadnezzar faces judgment even while his delusions of grandeur continue. He has another dream that features a tall tree that stands at the center of the world and is visible to all corners of the earths. Nebuchadnezzar describes the tree: "Its leaves were beautiful, its fruit abundant, and on it was food for all. Under it the wild animals found shelter, and the birds lived in its branches; from it every creature was fed" (v. 12). But the king's dream soon became a nightmare. A "holy one" came down from heaven and cried (vv. 14–16),

> Cut down the tree and trim off its branches; strip off its leaves and scatter its fruit. Let the animals flee from under it and the birds from its branches. But let the stump and its roots, bound with iron and bronze, remain in the ground, in the grass of the field. Let him be drenched with the dew of heaven, and let him live with the animals among the plants of the earth. Let his mind

be changed from that of a man and let him be given the mind of an animal, till seven times pass by for him.

When Daniel interprets this dream for the king, Daniel tells Nebuchadnezzar that the king himself is the tree, and that chopping it down and placing a band around it represents God's judgment on his kingdom. Nebuchadnezzar, Daniel says, will be made to act like an animal for seven years, to go on all fours in the dew and eat the grass of the earth: "You will be driven away from people and will live with the wild animals; you will eat grass like the ox and be drenched with the dew of heaven" (v. 25).

God's judgment on Nebuchadnezzar will be harsh, but Daniel reports that there is one way that Nebuchadnezzar can delay this judgment, one thing he must do to earn a stay from the God of the universe. What is this one thing? Is it to offer sacrifices? No. Is it to return to the temple the things that Nebuchadnezzar's men had stolen? No. To return God's people to their land? No. To bow down before Yahweh? Not exactly. Daniel tells Nebuchadnezzar that the only way Nebuchadnezzar can delay this judgment is to stop oppressing the poor. "Renounce your sins by doing what is right, and your wickedness by being kind to the oppressed" (4:27). Or as the New Living Translation puts it, "Stop sinning and do what is right. Break from your wicked past and be merciful to the poor." As the New American Standard Bible translates the verse, "Break away now from your sins by doing righteousness and from your iniquities by showing mercy to the poor." This last translation makes clear that Daniel is urging Nebuchadnezzar to break away from his sins *by* doing what is right and to break away from his iniquities *by* showing mercy to the poor. That is, showing mercy to the poor isn't something Nebuchadnezzar was to do in addition to breaking away from his iniquities, but it was a central practice to which Daniel was calling Nebuchadnezzar.

So what does this have to do with how we respond to poverty, distress, and vulnerability in urban life? This is a story about what it means to be human and what it means to truly be like God. Nebuchadnezzar wanted to be like God in having a kingdom that was forever and over all things. Daniel's message to Nebuchadnezzar was "You want to be like God in all the wrong, or at least inconsequential, ways. You want your kingdom to last forever and to be everywhere, but you should want to be like the God who loves and showers mercy on the poor. Anything less than that is subhuman, so if you can't do that, then you will face a fitting judgment. As an expression of your inability to embrace what it means to be human by caring for the poor, the distressed, the vulnerable, and the marginalized, you will live like an animal for seven years."

If we truly want to be like God, we should care for the least of these, providing shelter for the homeless, food for the hungry, and security to the vulnerable. We should empower the powerless and give voice to the voiceless. To do so is to be more like Jesus Christ, the true king who was not subhuman but perfectly human.

So what did I finally say when I spoke in the planning meeting? I tried to put Daniel 2–4 in a nutshell. Without a lot of research, I pointed out, it was hard for me to know whether it would be good for the low-income housing units to be in or out of the TIF district—each had its advantages and disadvantages. But I could know that God's Word teaches it is less than human to treat the poor with contempt, and for this reason we should consider the needs of the poor first. I could know that we are called to treat the vulnerable with love and mercy, to place the poor at the center of our concerns. I could know that this is the responsibility of our communities and their leaders—including secular authorities like the King of Babylon—and the church.

In the end, the municipality in question excluded the low-income housing units from the TIF initiative, leaving them just outside the district's boundaries. This increased the vulnerability of the community by putting them at high risk of displacement and afforded them no additional protections. Since then, and despite the activity of community members and many supporters, the refugees in that housing complex have experienced hardship upon hardship with no relief in sight. Many of us continue to lift them up in prayer to the One who came to inaugurate a kingdom that is good news for the poor (Luke 4:18).

"WANNA BE STARTIN'
SOMETHIN'?"

Shaping the Global Influence of Cities

I knew the Global Cities Summit would be a different sort of conference when speakers from Makkah (Mecca), London, Toronto, Nairobi, Shanghai, and Barcelona were followed by none other than Michael Jackson. Yes, that Michael Jackson. Between the opening plenary lecture and lunch, the sound system blasted the King of Pop's "Wanna Be Startin' Somethin'." Not your typical conference soundtrack. Then again, the Global Cities Summit was not your typical conference.[1]

The Summit brought together representatives of more than one hundred cities, along with planners, businesspeople, and others, to discuss the role of cities in addressing global challenges. How do global political, economic, and environmental issues affect cities? And just as importantly, how can cities address global issues? How is it that cities are related to the world around them? In a world in which cities are more important than ever to global affairs, how should they relate to the world?

This is a question faced by what we now call "global cities." Global cities are cities that are more directly linked to global economic, political, and cultural affairs, cities that in many ways bypass what has been a "nested" relationship with the nation-state since the mid-1600s. While most cities—Singapore, as a contemporary city-state, is the exception—still have their formal authority somehow limited by the nation-state, cities today have increased effective authority on the global stage. They have influence of the sort that has not been seen in cities since the early seventeenth century.

As we saw in chapter 3, cities not only have massive influence over even the farthest reaches of the global environment, generating approximately 80 percent of the greenhouse gases that are responsible for warming the planet and changing the climate, but cities are joining together in various transnational movements and networks to do something about climate change.[2] Cities also have massive economic influence. The World Bank, for example, has found that forty of the world's largest economies are cities.[3] The metabolism of cities—their inputs and outputs—has dramatic effects on far-off ecosystems, far-flung communities, and future generations.

In response to these developments, a movement that might be called "cosmopolitan urbanism" has arisen among cities best positioned to confront global challenges. Cosmopolitan urbanism represents the idea that, at the same time that they must address local challenges, cities can and should lead toward the common good on global challenges.[4]

The idea that cities should somehow account for and work toward the good of communities beyond their borders is not a new one. The Jewish philosopher Emanuel Levinas argued that "cities of refuge" provided the basis for what he described as a "humanitarian," or "humane," urbanism.[5] Recall that cities of refuge were places that welcomed strangers who were accused of killing their neighbor, and which provided the accused with a place of safety and refuge from judgment (Joshua 20). They were cities that were established and organized for the purpose of protecting people beyond the boundaries of their communities. Humane urbanism in this sense refers to cities that are shaped in such a way as to promote holistic human flourishing, not only for their residents but also for those beyond their borders.

Jewish ethicist Aryeh Cohen elaborates upon Levinas's idea by suggesting that humane urbanism is a "community of obligation" in which those who are not always in view, such as the homeless, the poor, and the working class, are nonetheless attended to and cared for.[6] Those who are not always in view? Who more represents those that are not always in view than those who are outside of the city but for whom the city's actions have major impacts?

The Christian theologian Edward Farley also gives us some ways of thinking about this same challenge. Farley suggests that social systems—and we might think of cities as spatial social systems—are either the sort that displace burdens onto others or absorb costs for others. According to Farley, social systems that displace costs onto others can be described as "subjugating" systems. Social systems that absorb costs for others can be described as "redemptive" systems.[7]

The question is what kind of community we want to become and live in. What kind of urban life do we want to lead? Do we want to live in the kinds of cities that seem to thrive while others bear burdens that make our prosperity possible? Or might our cities become the kinds of communities that liberate others, that bear their burdens, even when it costs us something? We should work toward communities that make it possible for others to flourish, even if it means having fewer goods ourselves. In other words, we might just become communities that are *for* other communities, like cities of refuge—cities that didn't only exist to serve themselves but existed to provide refuge to others in need. Cities of refuge existed to be for God and for others rather than only for themselves.

In this era of rising global influence of cities, in which cities are increasingly important to the individual lives of even non-urbanites all over the world, perhaps our cities too should be cities of refuge. This would have implications for how cities address their own challenges and whom they welcome into their communities. Our cities might become the kinds of places that promote the flourishing of others—sometimes by welcoming the strangers who come into our communities and sometimes by welcoming the burdens and costs of flourishing for others whom we may never see. If our cities were to become communities that embrace burdens in order that others may flourish, well, then we'd really be startin' somethin'.

CITIES OF TOMORROW
AND THE CITY OF GOD

Imagining the Future of Urban Life

I'm writing this next-to-last chapter from Greenline Coffee on the corner of 61st and Eberhart in Chicago's Woodlawn neighborhood, which is one of the city's most distressed communities. Almost a third of its households are below the poverty level. Nearly a fifth of adults do not have the advantage of a high school diploma. The unemployment rate is close to 20 percent. While crime of all sorts has been trending downward here for the past fifteen years, Woodlawn remains ranked among the city's most dangerous neighborhoods.

While these measures of distress represent an important dimension of urban life as experienced in Woodlawn today, they do not give a complete account of neighborhood life, and they don't represent a static and unchanging reality. Woodlawn has a rich history of prosperity and many assets with which to build a flourishing future. Neighborhoods change.

From my perch at this corner of Greenline, I can see evidence of this kind of change. Not long ago, when Woodlawn's population was at its peak in the 1960s, the abandoned lots and vacant buildings were sites of productive activity, part of a vibrant fabric of industrial, commercial, and residential life. Then, the neighborhood was home to more than 80,000 people. Now the population is roughly 23,000. Not far from here is a community garden on a lot that had previously been the site of a flourishing church congregation.

Through the window on the north side of Greenline, I see children passing east and west on 61st—nearly a third of the neighborhood's population is under eighteen years of age—and my prayers drift to the future of the neighborhood, to the cities of tomorrow. I'm not thinking of futurist accounts, either utopian or dystopian, that focus on massive, nonlinear, qualitative changes in our urban environments.[1] I'm thinking instead of the incremental but still meaningful changes that we make in our communities every day—changes that sometimes add up to big differences for a community. Indeed, Greenline itself may represent that kind of change. The business was founded by Sunshine Gospel Ministries, a community development organization that not only makes disciples through collaborations with local churches but also includes business-incubation projects that help the community to flourish economically. Neighborhoods change, and Greenline is part of that change.

Of course, whole cities change too. A once bustling town can become a ghost town. A backwater village can become a boomtown. Chicago is a city known for change. As Andrew Krmenec writes, "There is perhaps no North American city that has reinvented itself more than Chicago."[2] Over the course of just a few decades in the mid-1800s, Chicago went from what one author called a "pestilential swamp" to one of the fastest growing cities on the planet.[3] It became the financial center of the Midwest, the transportation hub of the United States, and, in Carl Sandburg's phrase, "hog butcher to the world" before global economic upheavals of the mid-1900s sent the city into decline. Since then, it has been in the process of reinventing itself as a global leader in the service economy.

Despite these changes, social relations in Chicago have been marked by the exploitation of vulnerable minority populations, from Native Americans to European immigrants, to blacks migrating mostly from the South of the country. Those who recognize what Janet Abu-Lughod describes as Chicago's "elegant façade and a deeply shadowed backstage"[4]—its glitzy downtown and its sometimes troubled but often unknown neighborhoods—might argue that the more things change in Chicago, the more they stay the same. How we see these changes depends upon our ability to see similarity in difference and difference in similarity.

This ability is also the key to relating the cities of tomorrow and the city to come. As our communities change, and as they differ one from another, we need to be able to affirm differences that matter while keeping in mind that all of them fall short of the kingdom of God. What we need is a way to distinguish between the cities of tomorrow—to admit that some of them are better than others—while admitting that none of them are the City of God. What we need is to balance two distinct forms of imagination: the analogical imagination and the dialectical imagination.[5]

In the first place, we must be able to imagine the ways in which the best of our human projects can approach the virtues of the kingdom of God, to discern similarities between the city of God and the cities we now inhabit. This discernment also enables us to differentiate one human project from another, to say that cities are more or less virtuous. To exercise this sort of imagination in urban life is to emphasize meaningful differences between cities and to envision the possibility of meaningful change that can come from the work of Christians and non-Christians alike.

At its best, this approach seems to authorize and empower participation in efforts toward real transformation, including planning, activism, and policy that bring about new and better cities of tomorrow. By measuring cities of tomorrow against the city to come, by saying that a city doesn't live up to its calling unless there is a sort of justice that resembles the justice of God, and by saying meaningful resemblance is possible, this imagination undermines complacency with a powerful prophetic potential. This mode of imagination lends a sense that we can "move the needle" in a meaningful direction: from "really far from the City of God" to "closer to the City of God."

At its worst, though, this approach undermines its own prophetic impulse. It risks treating imperfect human cities—and even the best of them are imperfect—as if they *are* the City of God. Thus, at its worst, it risks creating complacency. And what is most treacherous about this is the possibility that we would not continue to judge our cities, but rather might begin to idolize certain forms of human community. We might then seek to maintain our cities in their current form, rather than to subject our cities to searching critique. We might begin, as Jacques Ellul notes that we are wont to do with idols, to sacrifice people to our cities.[6] To authorize expectations of meaningful change, to justify meaningful discrimination between one city and another, to make sense of our recognition that meaningful change comes from the work of Christians and non-Christians alike, and to justify our own involvement in these works, we need to activate our ability to see similarity in difference, to imagine continuity. But we cannot afford to idolize our cities, even when they are at their best.

To chasten this impulse we must be able to imagine the infinite distance between the city to come and any human city. We must grasp "the reality of the infinite qualitative distinction between our cities and the cities of God."[7] We must be able to see difference despite similarity, to raise the standard of the New Jerusalem against even the most peaceful of human cities.

At its best, this sort of imagination helps us to tear down every idol. It has a powerfully apocalyptic impulse, inclined toward revealing the kingdom of God against all human works, demonstrating the frailty and feebleness of our efforts when stacked up against God's work. This sensibility empowers a critique so thorough and powerful that we are never at risk of idolizing the city or our efforts, of thinking that we're already there, of sacrificing people to maintain the order that we've already established in our urban life. It provides a platform for witnessing to the fact that God, and God alone, will deliver our cities, because it is clear that we cannot deliver them.

At its worst, though, this sort of imagination can seem to collapse all human efforts, including cities, into one category of efforts-that-simply-cannot-resemble-God's-work. This can leave us wondering, as David Tracy notes, "What hope remains for any similarity, any continuity, any order?"[8] Such hopelessness can devalue change and demotivate human work to make a difference in our communities. After all, if every city is equally distant from the ideal, if there is no continuity or resemblance, then what point is there in working? What point is there in trying to move the needle from "still infinitely distant from the City of God" to "infinitely distant from the City of God"?

The French social theorist and theologian Jacques Ellul is a good example of this approach. In Ellul's *The Meaning of the City*, he suggests that all human cities are equally marked by rebellion against God and that this rebellion is their defining feature.[9] According to Ellul, ever since Cain founded the first city, cities have represented humanity's greatest act of man's self-assertion and self-realization, and they are opposed to God's greatest accomplishment, Jesus Christ. Though God plans to redeem the city in the end—the real, human, fallen, cursed, and gritty city that we know—all of our efforts to improve the city amount to nothing of significance, because they cannot make the city honor God, and they cannot bring the city to express God's justice. Although Ellul would argue that we should remain involved with efforts to improve the city—if he did not believe this, it would be difficult to explain why he served for a time as deputy mayor of Bordeaux—he would also emphasize that we should expect little of consequence or significance to come of those efforts. Indeed, according to Ellul, the hallmark of our involvement is a sense of humor—a lightheartedness about our human efforts that comes from understanding how little they will accomplish and that, in turn, exalts the God who will accomplish so much more in the end. Ellul called his own position "active pessimism." Active in the sense of always working; pessimistic in the sense of not expecting the work to amount to much.

This approach challenges us to "face the reality of the really new, the *novum*, and the future breaking in and confronting every present, exploding every complacency . . . [and] to remember the eschatological 'not yet' in every incarnational 'always-already' and even every 'but-even-now'; resurrectional transformation."[10] It relativizes every human accomplishment, no matter how noble. It reveals the contours of the City of God in contrast to all human cities. Its advantage is that it cannot possibly lose its ability to say that human cities have fallen short of their calling as communities. It can always empower us to note how far short a community has fallen—each one is just infinitely short in its own way. Its disadvantage is that it quickly loses its ability to emphasize that some communities are thriving in ways that others are not, that some changes are meaningful and good, and that we should not only be involved in change, but we should expect that change to matter.

If Christians are to contribute to thriving cities, then we must cultivate both of these approaches. We must strike a balance between prophetic and apocalyptic sensibilities. This balance is something we must recover if we are to emphasize both the real and important differences between one city and another—between neighborhoods that undermine human flourishing and neighborhoods that promote it—as well as the real and important differences between even our most thriving neighborhoods and the city that we hope for, the city that God will build.

We need to ask God to grant us this balance if we want to

understand how a zero-brownfields future might matter and why we should work toward it even though we know that future remains infinitely distant from the glory of the New Jerusalem. We need to seek this balance if we want to understand how a city that treats the poor with dignity and puts them at the center of their community is a good thing but still falls short of the new creation. We need to find this balance if we are not to confuse our hope in the cities of tomorrow with our hope in the city to come.

Here at Greenline Coffee, I'm praying for some imagination. And I'm praying for some balance.

FOR FLOURISHING COMMUNITIES AND FAITHFUL URBAN LIFE

A Prayer for Future Cities

In the time it has taken to read this book—depending on how quickly you've done that—the world's urban population has probably grown by dozens, if not hundreds, of thousands. From the Nigerian countryside, people have been streaming into Lagos with the expectation of peace. From every corner of the world, people have been flying into London with visions of opportunity. In every city, children have been born in hope of a flourishing urban world that more and more resembles the new creation.

At the same time, cities confront us every day with dream-crushing violence and vulnerability, the yawning chasm between what is and what should be, the distressing gulf between the ideals and realities of urban life. In the time it has taken to read this book, slums have swollen to record proportions. From New York to Nairobi, communities have experienced pollution, prejudice, and poverty.

Urban life is full of promise and fraught with peril, and it is in this ambiguity that we must seek the welfare of our cities. Both poles of this reality call us to action, highlighting desperate need and great potential, inviting us to transform our cities into communities of peace and justice.

When we act, however, we begin to understand both the possibilities and the limitations of urban transformation. We realize the fragility of even the greatest of human achievements. We begin to understand our own limits. If we're honest about our finitude, we have to admit that we can't do it all. If we're honest about our fallenness, we know that we sometimes don't want to.

Recognizing our finitude and our fallenness can be a dark moment—a moment in which we sense the frailty of our independence, ambition, and determination—but it should also be an occasion for prayer. The gap between what we desire and what we do, or between what we desire and what we *should desire*, should drive us to express our dependence on God, who will put everything right in his time and enable our participation in his work even now. We depend on God to make us more and more like Jesus Christ, more and more the images of God that we were made to be. Prayer is an expression of this dependence on God. And whatever we are called to in the city, whether it succeeds or fails, we are called to prayer.

So let us close with a reading from the *Book of Common Prayer*. "For Cities" reminds us of our hope in a God who will one day establish a flourishing city and even now enables our faithful urban life. "For Cities" petitions God to renew our cities, to empower us to participate in that renewal, and to make us, through that work, more fully human. There can no more fitting way to conclude our reflections than to pray together.

> Heavenly Father, in your Word you have given us a vision of that Holy City to which the nations of the world bring their glory: Behold and visit, we pray, the cities of the earth. Renew the ties of mutual regard which form our civic life. Send us honest and able leaders. Enable us to eliminate poverty, prejudice,

and oppression, that peace may prevail with righteousness, and justice with order, and that men and women from different cultures and with differing talents may find with one another the fulfillment of their humanity; through Jesus Christ our Lord. *Amen.*[1]

ACKNOWLEDGMENTS

I would like to thank my friend and colleague Gene Green for bringing me into conversations about the Ordinary Theology Series and for soliciting this volume. Gene's guidance, along with feedback from Madison Trammel and Bob Hudson at Zondervan, has been very helpful. Finally, and most importantly, many thanks are due to my wife, Becky, and to our children, Joe, Ben, and Rose, for their patience as I devoted time to this project.

NOTES

Foreword to the Ordinary Theology Series

1. John MacKay, *A Preface to Christian Theology* (New York: Macmillan, 1941), 27.

Chapter 1: What Has Chicago to Do with Jerusalem?

1. Tertullian, *"De praescriptione haereticorum,"* in *Early Latin Theology: Selections from Tertullian, Cyprian, Ambrose, and Jerome*, ed. S. L. Greenslade (Louisville, KY: Westminster, 1956).

2. Richard Florida, "Foreword," in the *Atlas of Cities*, ed. Paul Knox (Princeton: Princeton University Press, 2014), 8.

3. Noah Toly, "Introduction to the Theme Issue," in "Christian Perspectives on 'the City,'" special issue, *Christian Scholar's Review* 38, no. 4, ed. Noah Toly (2009).

4. For an interpretation of Deuteronomy 6:4–5 that emphasizes this implication of 6:5 by way of suggestion that "heart," "soul," and "strength" represent sorts of concentric circles from which no part of a life can be excluded, see Daniel I. Block, "How Many Is God? An Investigation into the Meaning of Deuteronomy 6:4–5," *Journal of the Evangelical Theological Society* 47, no. 2, (2004): 193–212.

5. Abraham Kuyper, "Sphere Sovereignty," in *Abraham Kuyper: A Centennial Reader*, ed. James D. Bratt (Grand Rapids: Eerdmans, 1998), 488.

6. Beth Jones, *Practicing Christian Doctrine: An Introduction to Thinking and Living Theologically* (Grand Rapids: Baker, 2014).

Chapter 2: Encountering Cities

1. United Nations Department of Economic and Social Affairs, *Demographic Yearbook: 1998* (New York: United Nations, 2000). Because the city's populous peri-urban slums were very likely underrepresented in official counts, the population of the city was probably much closer to 20 million than the 16 million listed in the record books.

2. For background on *flânerie*, see Frederic Gros, *A Philosophy of Walking* (New York: Verso, 2014); Walter Benjamin, *The Arcades Project* (Boston: Belknap, 2002).

3. Jacques Ellul, *The Meaning of the City* (Grand Rapids: Eerdmans, 1970); T. J. Gorringe, *A Theology of the Built Environment: Justice, Empowerment, Redemption* (Cambridge: Cambridge University Press, 2002); Mark Gornik, *To Live in Peace: Biblical Faith and the Changing Inner City* (Grand Rapids: Eerdmans, 2002); Philip Sheldrake, *Spiritual City: Theology, Spirituality, and the Urban* (New York: Wiley-Blackwell, 2014).

4. Those interested in urban ministry books might consult Harvie M. Conn and Manuel Ortiz, *Urban Ministry: The Kingdom, the City, and the People of God* (Downers Grove, IL: InterVarsity, 2001); Timothy Keller, *Center Church: Doing Balanced, Gospel-Centered Ministry in Your City* (Grand Rapids: Zondervan, 2012); Eric Swanson, Sam Williams, and Reggie McNeal, *To Transform a City: Whole Church, Whole Gospel, Whole City* (Grand Rapids: Zondervan, 2010).

5. Readers interested in my thoughts on violent crime in Chicago should consult my blog at http://www.noahtoly.com.

6. This is, admittedly, not all that should be said on the matter of theological anthropology. Nor will we cover here everything that could be said about this approach to theological anthropology.

7. For an account of the swelling demographics of cities around the world, see Doug Saunders, *Arrival City: How the Largest Migration in History Is Reshaping Our World* (New York: Vintage, 2012).

Chapter 3: Zero Brownfields Future

1. John Byrne et al., *The Brownfields Challenge: A Survey of Environmental Justice and Community Participation Initiatives among Ten National Brownfield Pilot Projects; A Report Prepared for the Delaware General Assembly* (Newark, Delaware: Center for Energy and Environmental

Policy, 1999); John Byrne et al., "Community Participation Is Key
to Environmental Justice in Brownfields," in *Race, Poverty, and the
Environment* 3, no. 1 (2001): 6–7; Environmental Protection Agency,
"Brownfields and Land Revitalization" (Washington, DC: EPA), accessed
at http://www.epa.gov/brownfields.

2. Nicholas Wolterstorff, *Art in Action* (Carlisle: Paternoster, 1997), 82.

3. See William Cronon, *Nature's Metropolis: Chicago and the Great West*
(New York: Norton, 1991). See also Noel Castree, "Environmental
Issues: From Policy to Political Economy," *Progress in Human
Geography: An International Review of Geographical Work in the Social
Sciences and Humanities* 26, no. 3 (2002): 357–65; Joel Tarr, *Devastation
and Renewal: An Environmental History of Pittsburgh and Its Region*
(Pittsburgh: University of Pittsburgh Press, 2005); Joel Tarr, *The Search
for the Ultimate Sink: Urban Pollution in Historical Perspective* (Akron:
University of Akron Press, 2011); David Soll, *Empire of Water: An
Environmental and Political History of the New York City Water Supply*
(Ithaca: Cornell University Press, 2013); Harold L. Platt, *Shock Cities:
The Environmental Transformation and Reform of Manchester and
Chicago* (Chicago: University of Chicago Press, 2005).

4. Naison D. Mutigwa-Mangiza et al., *Cities and Climate Change: Global
Report on Human Settlements 2011* (Washington, DC: Earthscan, 2011).
For more on cities and climate change, see also Matthew E. Kahn,
Climatopolis: How Our Cities Will Thrive in the Hotter Future (New
York: Basic Books, 2010).

5. Ebenezer Howard, *Garden Cities of To-Morrow* (London:
Sonnenschein, 1902).

6. Daniel I. Block, "To Serve and to Keep: Toward a Biblical
Understanding of Humanity's Responsibility in the Face of the
Biodiversity Crisis," in *Keeping God's Earth: The Global Environment
in Biblical Perspective*, ed. Noah J. Toly and Daniel I. Block (Downers
Grove, IL: InterVarsity, 2010), 116–42.

7. In *Good and Evil: Interpreting a Human Condition* (Minneapolis:
Fortress, 1990), Edward Farley suggests that the entanglement of "the
conditions of well-being" with "challenge, frustration, and limitation" is
the "tragic" element of the human condition.

8. In this quote Bauckham does explore the reasons that this combination
was "not a problem" before the fall and the curse. Those reasons,
whether attributable to finitude or fallenness or both, are worth
exploring but cannot be examined at length here.

9. Richard Bauckham, *The Bible and Ecology: Rediscovering the Community of Creation* (Waco: Baylor University Press, 2010), 107. Citing Evan Eisenberg, *The Ecology of Eden* (London: Picador, 1998), xix.

10. See, for example, Edward Glaeser, *The Triumph of the City: How Our Greatest Invention Makes Us Richer, Smarter, Greener, Healthier, and Happier* (New York: Penguin, 2012).

11. David Owen, *Green Metropolis: Why Living Smaller, Living Closer, and Driving Less Are the Keys to Sustainability* (New York: Riverhead, 2010).

Chapter 4: The Shape of Community

1. Terry Straus, ed., *Native Chicago* (Chicago: Albatross Press, 2002).

2. Amanda Seligman, "Uptown," in the *Encyclopedia of Chicago* (Chicago: University of Chicago Press, 2004), 847–48. See also Todd Gitlin and Nanci Hollander, *Uptown: Poor Whites in Chicago* (New York: Harper & Row, 1970); Marty Hansen, *Behind the Golden Door: Refugees in Uptown* (Chicago: H. H. Publications, 1991); Elizabeth Warren, *Chicago's Uptown: Public Policy, Neighborhood Decay, and Citizen Action in an Urban Community* (Chicago: Loyola University Press, 1979).

3. For a treatment of the ways in which global dynamics, local contexts, and municipal policy intersect to shape neighborhoods and cities, see Janet Abu-Lughod, *New York, Chicago, Los Angeles: America's Global Cities* (Minneapolis: University of Minnesota Press, 2000).

4. For the origins of the term, see Doug Saunders, *Arrival City: How the Largest Migration in History Is Reshaping Our World* (New York: Vintage, 2012).

5. James R. Grossman, "African-American Migration to Chicago," in *Ethnic Chicago: A Multicultural Portrait*, ed. Melvin G. Holli and Peter d'A. Jones (Grand Rapids: Eerdmans, 1995). See also Janet Abu-Lughod, *New York, Chicago, Los Angeles: America's Global Cities* (Minneapolis: University of Minnesota Press, 2000).

6. Daniel Brook, *A History of Future Cities* (New York: Norton, 2013).

7. For an exploration of the ways in which new technologies make long-term adjustment, and not just moving, easier for immigrant populations, see Elizabeth M. Aranda, Sallie Hughes, and Elena Sabogal, *Making a Life in Multiethnic Miami: Immigration and the Rise of a Global City* (Boulder: Lynne Rienner Publishers, 2014).

8. Gordon Mathews, *Ghetto at the Center of the World: Chungking Mansions, Hong Kong* (Chicago: University of Chicago Press, 2011).

9. William McNeill, "Cities and Their Consequences," *The American Interest: Policy, Politics, and Culture* 2, no. 4 (March/April 2007): 5–12.

10. Andrew Lynn, "Do Cities Tear Us Apart?" at *Common Place: The Anatomy and the Art of Thriving Communities*, July 11, 2014. Available at http://iasc-culture.org/THR/channels/Common_Place/2014/07/do-cities-tear-us-apart/.

11. Jane Jacobs, *The Death and Life of Great American Cities* (New York: Modern Library, 2011); Lewis Mumford, *The City in History: Its Origins, Its Transformations, and Its Prospects* (New York: Mariner, 1968).

12. William H. Whyte, *The Social Life of Small Urban Spaces* (New York: Project for Public Spaces, 2001).

13. Wolf Krötke, "The Humanity of the Human Person in Karl Barth's Anthropology," in *The Cambridge Companion to Karl Barth*, ed. John Webster (Cambridge: Cambridge University Press, 2000), 168. See also Karl Barth, *Church Dogmatics* II/2 (Edinburgh: T&T Clark, 1957), 220ff.

14. Margaret M. Mitchell, "Reconciliation: Biblical Reflections: III. Paul's 1 Corinthians and Reconciliation in the Church: Promises and Pitfalls," *New Theology Review: A Catholic Journal of Theology and Ministry* 10, no. 2 (1997): 39–49. See also Margaret M. Mitchell, *Paul and the Rhetoric of Reconciliation: An Exegetical Investigation of the Language and Composition of 1 Corinthians* (Louisville: Westminster John Knox, 1993).

Chapter 5: Caring for the Least of These

1. Mike Davis, *Planet of Slums* (New York: Verso, 2006).

Chapter 6: "Wanna Be Startin' Somethin'?"

1. This opening paragraph is taken from Noah Toly, "Postcard from the Global Cities Summit," *Comment: Public Theology for the Common Good* (2014), accessed at http://www.cardus.ca/comment/article/4237/a-postcard-from-the-global-cities-summit/.

2. See Sofie Bouteligier, *Cities, Networks, and Global Environmental Governance: Spaces of Innovation, Places of Leadership* (New York: Routledge, 2012). See also Noah J. Toly, "Transnational Municipal Networks in Climate Politics: From Global Governance to Global Politics," *Globalizations* 5, no. 3 (2008): 341–56.

3. Daniel P. Hoornweg et al., *Cities and Climate Change: An Urgent Agenda* (New York: World Bank, 2010).

4. See, for example, Benjamin R. Barber, *If Mayors Ruled the World: Dysfunctional Nations, Rising Cities* (New Haven: Yale University Press, 2013). See also Noah Toly, "The Magic of Mayors?" *Comment: Public Theology for the Common Good* (Summer 2014), 57–63.

5. Emanuel Levinas, "Cities of Refuge (Extract from the Tractate Makkoth 10a)," in *Beyond the Verse: Talmudic Readings and Lectures* (London: Athlone Press, 1994).

6. Aryeh Cohen, *Justice in the City: An Argument from the Sources of Rabbinic Judaism* (Brighton, MA: Academic Studies Press, 2012).

7. Edward Farley, *Good and Evil: Interpreting a Human Condition* (Minneapolis: Fortress, 1990).

Chapter 7: Cities of Tomorrow and the City of God

1. Those sorts of accounts are actually quite interesting and even very helpful. For analysis of what we can learn from these accounts, see Robert Warren, Stacy Warren, Samuel Nunn, and Colin Warren, "The Future of the Future in Planning: Appropriating Cyberpunk Visions of the City," *Journal of Planning Education and Research* 18 (1998): 49–60.

2. Andrew J. Krmenec, "Chicago: Transportation and Trade Gateway to the Midwest," in *Chicago's Geographies: Metropolis for the 21st Century*, eds. Richard P. Greene, Mark J. Bouman, and Dennis Grammenos (Washington, DC: Association of American Geographers, 2006), 87–102.

3. *Chicago: City of the Century*, DVD, directed by Austin Hoyt and Patricia Garcia Rios (Boston and Chicago: WGBH Educational Foundation and WTTW, 2003).

4. Janet Abu-Lughod, *New York, Chicago, Los Angeles: America's Global Cities* (Minneapolis: University of Minnesota Press, 2000).

5. This chapter draws loosely upon the work of David Tracy in *The Analogical Imagination: Christian Theology and the Culture of Pluralism* (New York: Crossroad, 1981). See pages 415–21 for Tracy's discussion of the relationship between analogical and dialectical ways of thinking.

6. Jacques Ellul, "Christian Faith and Social Reality," in *Sources and Trajectories: Eight Early Articles by Jacques Ellul That Set the Stage*, ed. Marva Dawn (Grand Rapids: Eerdmans, 1997).

7. Tracy, *The Analogical Imagination*, 415.

8. Tracy, *The Analogical Imagination*, 417.

9. Jacques Ellul, *The Meaning of the City* (Grand Rapids: Eerdmans, 1970).

10. Tracy, *The Analogical Imagination*, 265–66.

Chapter 8: For Flourishing Communities and Faithful Urban Life

1. *The Book of Common Prayer* (New York: Oxford University Press, 1990), 825.

Scalpel and the Cross
A Theology of Surgery

Gene L. Green

We know the bedrock themes upon which the Christian faith stands: creation, fall, redemption, restoration. As Christians, we live within these great moments of God's plan for humanity and all of his creation. In other words, our lives are part of Christian theology—every part of our lives, even surgery.

As a part of Zondervan's Ordinary Theology Series, *The Scalpel and the Cross* recounts New Testament professor Gene Green's encounter with open-heart surgery and carefully examines the many ways in which Christian doctrine spoke into the experience. The result is a short book that avoids shallow explanations and glib promises, instead guiding readers to a deeper understanding and an enduring hope in the face of one of modern life's necessary traumas.

Available in stores and online!

Political Disciple
A Theology of Public Life

Vincent Bacote;
Gene L. Green, Series Editor

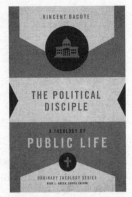

What might it mean for public and political life to be understood as an important
dimension of following Jesus? As a part of
Zondervan's Ordinary Theology Series,
Vincent E. Bacote's *The Political Disciple* addresses this question by considering not only whether Christians have (or need)
permission to engage the public square, but also what it means
to reflect Christlikeness in our public practice, as well as what to
make of the typically slow rate of social change and the tension
between relative allegiance to a nation and/or a political party
and ultimate allegiance to Christ. Pastors, laypeople, and college students will find this concise volume a handy primer on
Christianity and public life.

Available in stores and online!

Faithful
A Theology of Sex

Beth Felker Jones;
Gene L. Green, Series Editor

Many believers accept traditional Christian sexual morality but have very little idea why it matters for the Christian life. In *Faithful*, author Beth Felker Jones sketches a theology of sexuality that demonstrates sex is not about legalistic morals with no basis in reality but rather about the God who is faithful to us.

In Hosea 2:19–20 God says to Israel, "I will take you for my wife forever; I will take you for my wife in righteousness and in justice, in steadfast love, and in mercy. I will take you for my wife in faithfulness; and you shall know the Lord." This short book explores the goodness of sexuality as created and redeemed, and it suggests ways to navigate the difficulties of living in a world in which sexuality, like everything else, suffers the effects of the fall.

As part of Zondervan's Ordinary Theology Series, *Faithful* takes a deeper look at a subject Christians talk about often but not always thoughtfully. This short, insightful reflection explores the deeper significance of the body and sexuality.

Available in stores and online!